# Restoring the Ark of the Covenant to His Church

*God's Manifest Presence*

By: Rose Mowriyah Shivambo

# Copyright Information

<u>Bringing Back the Ark of the Covenant to His Church</u>
*God's Manifest Presence*
by: Rose Mowriyah Shivambo

All scripture quotations are from:
New International Version (NIV)
New King James Version (NKJV)
New American Standard Bible (NASB)

Copyright © 2017 by
Good News Fellowship Ministries
220 Sleepy Creek Rd.
Macon, GA 31210
ISBN: 978-1-888081-27-5

No part of this book may be reproduced or transmitted in any form or by any means, electronic or mechanical, including photocopying, recording, or by an information storage and retrieval system, without permission in writing from the Author.

Cover Designed and Formatting Lisa Walters Buck

# Table of Contents

| | |
|---|---|
| Dedication | i |
| Acknowledgments | iii |
| Introduction | 1 |
| Chapter 1 | 7 |
| YOU ARE THE LORD GOD'S SANCTUARY | |
| Chapter 2 | 13 |
| THE PLACE OF THE PRESENCE | |
| Chapter 3 | 23 |
| THE PRESS AND THE FIRE | |
| Chapter 4 | 29 |
| HIS HOLY SPIRIT | |
| Chapter 5 | 37 |
| HOLINESS OF GOD | |
| Chapter 6 | 41 |
| HIS DEEP LOVE | |
| Chapter 7 | 51 |
| WORSHIP | |
| Chapter 8 | 57 |
| GOD'S MANIFEST PRESENCE | |
| Chapter 9 | 63 |
| POWER OF GOD | |
| Chapter 10 | 67 |
| THE IDENTITY OF THE CHURCH IN CHRIST JESUS | |
| Prayer for the Church | 71 |
| About the Author | 73 |

# Dedication

This book is dedicated to my loving mother Mary, whose Godly ways were instilled in me from birth, and have always been accompanied by her fervent prayers.

To all my siblings, Catherine, Pamela, Paul, Harrison, Margaret, Rodah, and Hope. Each day with you is special. You are a blessing from above!

And to the entire Church of Christ that awaits His coming. What a joy it shall be!

# Acknowledgments

One of the most beautiful things in my life, that I bless the Lord Jesus Christ for every single day, is not just salvation, but also growing in His revelation. Knowing Him each day is a journey of wonderful encounters. I can't trade His love for anything! My loving mother, Mary, is a unique figure in my life. Her prayers have always built my life up. I also want to express my sincere gratitude to my spiritual mentors. The Lord has always brought the right ones to me. Bishop Charles Mulema, Rev. Simon Muasya, Rev. Ken Monyoncho of Nairobi Gospel Centers International, and Bishop Okoji Ndukwe, and Pastor Bose Ndukwe of Soul Reapers Worship Center International. Some planted, others water, but all have made me grow into a woman of substance. May God bless you all abundantly!

To all my spiritual friends that the Lord has brought in my life. What can I say? Many of you have turned out to be a great blessing. You have challenged my spiritual life by making me get into the Lord's depths. I love you amazingly. None of this would have been fruitful if my close family and many in the Body of Christ didn't stand with me in prayer.

My special thanks to my editors who dedicated their time, knowledge, and wisdom to make this a reality. I bless the Lord for you.

# Introduction

The Ark of the Covenant represents the fullness of God in man. It was also called the "Ark of Witness" because when filled with His presence we witness, having gone through the outer and inner courts of the Temple. One who has entered the Holy of Holies with his God speaks the very words of God and God's nature is evidently working through him.

The Ark of the Covenant is the presence of God dwelling within, upon, and around God's people. The Church of Christ (or the Body/Bride of Christ) is God's Temple -- a holy sanctuary where the Lord God dwells through His Spirit (1 Corinthians 3:16). But the presence of God will not dwell in unclean and defiled vessels. The Lord God was objective to any uncleanness in the camp. He commanded Moses to tell His people to have a clean and holy camp so that He would not see anything indecent among them and turn away from them (Deuteronomy 23:23).

When the Lord said to me, "Go and take back the Ark of the Covenant to My Church," I sought Him for revelation, until I came to an understanding that His presence is not in His church. The church is on its own while the Ark of the Covenant, which is God's presence, is somewhere else. How can the branch grow on its own when disconnected from the true vine? (John 15:5)

It was the Ark of the Covenant in the times of Noah (Genesis 6:18), and only those who entered the Ark were saved. Even today, it is still the Ark of the Covenant, (Jesus Christ - the Lord Himself) and as we, His saints, walk daily with Him and learn obedience to the Father, will be allowed to enter in. This can only happen when we remain in Him and He in us (John 15: 4-5). When the Church loses her closeness with the Lord, she loses God's presence.

There were three graces put in the Ark of the Covenant: The Ten Commandments, the Pot of Manna, and the Rod of Aaron that budded. If the Bride of Christ misunderstands these, then she won't be able to be formed into a holy sanctuary. How will she be formed without submitting to His authority, His will, obeying His word, and feeding on His body and blood for daily strength? If she is not formed, how will His Holy presence dwell within her? If His presence doesn't dwell in her, how will she reflect His glory? She desperately needs these: Obedience to God's authority, God's Will, God's Word, and His Holy Spirit.

## *The Pot of Manna*

Jesus is the Bread of Life. Those who eat of His "flesh" shall live (John 6:3). The Church of Christ must fully remain in the Lord. If she disconnects, she will lack supply. She can only grow if she feeds and drinks the right spiritual foods: His word and His Holy Spirit.

There is no other food for the body of Christ apart from His own "flesh and blood". We must "feed" on Him and "drink" of Him daily. The children of God, the Israelites, were instructed to feed on fresh manna each day. Yesterday's anointing cannot carry you through today. The church is supposed to feed on the Word of God daily for strength and growth (1 Peter 2:2).

## *The Rod of Aaron That Budded*

The Lord Jesus Christ is the High Priest and ultimate authority. He submitted under the authority of His Father by saying yes to His will (John 12:27-28).

The Lord is calling the Church to submit to His authority. We have been created to live His will. Failing to fulfill His will on earth means we haven't submitted to His plan, will, and calling upon us. When we accomplish the Father's will, we bring Him glory.

No one can walk with God and obey His voice without surrender. The Lord told Peter:

> *"Very truly I tell you, when you were younger you dressed yourself and went where you wanted; but when you are old you will stretch out your hands, and someone else will dress you and lead you where you do not want to go." - John 21:18*

We must submit under His authority. We must choose to trust Him and to follow His leading, regardless of where He leads us.

## *The Testimony*

Jesus Christ did not reject God's standard of living. He obeyed God's law and lived a sinless life. His sacrifice instituted a new covenant that was not based on the Law, but pure righteousness from God that comes through faith in Jesus Christ to all who believe.

It took obedience for Him to accomplish this. Saying yes to Jesus at salvation is one thing, but following Jesus daily is another thing. It is in following Him that we obey His voice. The Lord says;

> *"My sheep listen to My voice; I know them, and they follow Me. I give them eternal life, and they*

*shall never perish; no one will snatch them out of My hand." - John 10:27-28*

For His church to get hold of eternal life, she must follow Him daily in submission to His will and authority as she feeds on the word of life that He gives.

# Chapter 1

## *You are the Lord God's Sanctuary*

*I will not enter my house or go to my bed. I will allow no sleep to my eyes, no slumber to my eyelids, till I find a place for the Lord, a dwelling for the Mighty One of Jacob. - Psalm 132:3-5*

Do you know that you are positioned as God's temple in Christ Jesus? (1 Corinthians 3:16) Do you understand that building is taking place practically? (1 Peter 2:5) We are God's Temple and He lives within us through His Spirit (1 Corinthians 3:16). The Lord does not dwell in houses made with hands. The Lord commanded Moses to tell the Israelites to bring offerings so that they would build Him a sanctuary where He would dwell among them. *Note that the Lord was specific on the offerings that were to be brought.* The Lord told Moses to speak to Israelites, but only those whose hearts prompted them were to bring the offerings. He was specific on the pattern in which the sanctuary was to be built. He wanted it made exactly as He showed to Moses.

> *The LORD said to Moses, $^2$"Tell the Israelites to bring Me an offering. You are to receive the offering for Me from everyone whose heart prompts them to give. $^3$These are the offerings you are to receive from them: gold, silver and bronze; $^4$blue, purple and scarlet yarn and fine linen; goat hair; $^5$ram skins dyed red and another type of durable leather[a]; acacia wood; $^6$olive oil for the light; spices for the anointing oil and for the fragrant incense; $^7$and onyx stones and other gems to be mounted on the ephod and breast-piece. $^8$Then have them make a sanctuary for me, and I will dwell among them. $^9$Make this tabernacle and all its furnishings exactly like the pattern I will show you." - Exodus 25:1-9*

This is key to the Church today. It takes a willing heart that will surrender and yield to the Spirit of God, to be built into a holy sanctuary.

> *You also, like living stones, are being built into a spiritual house to be a holy priesthood, offering spiritual sacrifices acceptable to God through Jesus Christ." - 1 Peter 2:5*

Hallelujah!

For this temple to be constructed with the exact materials that God desires, and for this temple to be constructed exactly in the pattern the Lord desires, the Church needs to be nowhere else other than in His presence seeking to hear what the Spirit says to her. The Lord has set His foundation on His holy mountain (Psalm 87:1). If He is the foundation that His Church must be built on, then she must dwell in His presence. It is key to have a willing heart to hear Him and to see what He reveals to you. The Ark of the Covenant was specifically placed in the Holy of Holies. If the Ark of the Covenant is to be formed within the Church, then she must be willing to be built into a holy sanctuary. When the prophet Jeremiah was sent to the potter's house, he found the potter working at the wheel. The pot he was shaping from the clay was marred in his hands, so he formed it into another pot, shaping it as seemed best to him. The Lord said to the prophet,

> *"Can I not do with you, Israel, as this potter does?" Declares the LORD. "Like clay in the hand of the potter, so are you in my hand, Israel." - Jeremiah 18:5-10*

This remarking calls for total surrender. If only His Church can get to the place of surrender, then the Lord will have His way in her life.

The Church of Christ is busy building her own house while the house of the Lord is in ruins (Haggai 1:4). She is busy feeding and nourishing the flesh while the spirit starves. The Lord dwells in our spirit-man. Where will the Lord find His dwelling? We must feed the spirit-man with spiritual foods. This food can only be found in God's presence. God commanded Haggai to tell His people to build Him a sanctuary so that He could have a dwelling place.

> *"Go up into the mountains and bring down timber and build my house, so that I may take pleasure in it and be honored," says the LORD. - Haggai 1:8*

It's clear that God's presence resided on the mountain. His presence is the only place from where we can feed our spirit-man. We must get back to the place of the presence.

Why has His Church departed from His presence? David says it marvelously. He was a man after God's own heart. This is what made him declare these words,

> *[3]I will not enter my house or go to my bed, [4]I will allow no sleep to my eyes or slumber to my eyelids, [5]till I find a place for the LORD, a dwelling for the Mighty One of Jacob. - Psalm 132:3-5*

If His Church has this desire, the Lord will have a dwelling place. The Ark of the Covenant will not reside out of us - His Church. It's when King Solomon finished building and furnishing God's house that he and the priests brought in the Ark of the Covenant of the Lord to its place - into the inner sanctuary of the temple, to the Most Holy Place (1 Kings 8:6).

Then King Solomon said,

*I have indeed built you a magnificent temple for you, a place for you to DWELL forever. - 1 Kings 8:13*

The Church of Christ has denied herself the best part. She has not let the Lord in to dwell in her. She is on her own; even though she still has the name "Christian". She has not allowed the Lord to mold her. She is still running away from the making process.

This is the very reason why God's presence is left with no dwelling place in His Church. David understood that the only thing he couldn't lose was the Lord's presence. He asked the Lord not to cast him from His presence, or take His Holy Spirit from him" (Psalms 51:11). The Church needs to come back to the place of the presence, so that she can be made into a holy and operating vessel -- a temple where God's presence can dwell.

# Chapter 2
## *The Place of the Presence*

*One thing I ask of the Lord, this is what I seek: that I may dwell in the house of the Lord all the days of my life, to gaze upon the beauty of the Lord and to seek Him in His temple. - Psalm 27:4*

When you lose the place of the presence, you lose His presence. You can still get back, but it is not easy. It will cost you dearly. You don't want to go through this. You must guard the secret place passionately. Key people in Scripture such as Mary Magdalene, Hannah, Ruth, and many others understood that they had to dwell in the place of His presence. They chose to be closer to the Lord by keeping in His presence. Once there, do not depart! Do not just visit! You must dwell. This is where every Christian draws the waters of life. While Orpah kissed her mother-in-law good-bye, Ruth clung to her. She said to Naomi,

*Where you go I will go, and where you stay I will stay. Your people will be my people, and your God*

*my God. Where you die, I will die, and there I will be buried. - Ruth 1:14, 16-17*

While Penninah enjoyed her temporal blessings, Hannah chose to keep in God's presence for conception (1 Samuel 1). While the two disciples went back to their homes after viewing the empty tomb, Mary Magdaline chose to stay back in God's presence to seek the face of the Lord (John 20). The place of the presence can never be far away from you. The Lord God said to Jeremiah,

*For as a belt is bound around a man's waist, so I bound the whole house of Israel and Judah to Me, to be My people for my renown and praise and honor. - Jeremiah 13:11*

Many have abandoned this precious place. They have no idea what is offered in this place. It's only a dead Church that works itself away from the place of the presence. While Martha was being distracted with so many things in the name of serving, Mary was seated at the feet of Jesus. The Lord said Mary had chosen the better thing that was needed (Luke 10:42), which was sitting at His feet.

This is the very place where we meet and commune with the Lord in order to get to know the Lord personally, to rest in the Lord's love, and to fully depend on the Lord. It is here that we tap into the Lord's peace and joy and our desires and longings are for the Lord. Our calling and purpose sets us on fire and nothing else will satisfy us. In this place we need nothing else but the Lord. We unveil His depths. We are sanctified, cleansed and purified, and we are transformed into His likeness. We have total intimacy with Him. It is a place of impartation and the place where we bear the most fruit.

It will always cost us to camp in God's presence. Yes, the cost is not cheap; but the treasure we find in His presence is incomparable.

Elisha had to burn the yoke and slaughter his oxen to be in God's presence. And even this was not enough, he had to kiss his parents good-bye in order to follow Elijah to the end (1 Kings 19:19-21).

When Elijah said to Elisha, "Stay here; for the Lord has sent me to Bethel." Elisha replied, "As surely as the Lord lives and as you live, I will not leave you." It happened from Gilgal to Bethel to Jericho to Jordan. Moreover, Elisha encountered distractions.

The company of prophets along the way asked him, "Do you know that the Lord is going to take your master from you today?" But Elisha replied, "I know, but do not speak of it." Indeed, the treasure awaited. When he asked of the double portion of Elijah's spirit, Elijah said, "You have asked for a hard thing!" But because Elisha was in God's presence at that very moment, he was able to receive it (2 Kings 2). If we only visit or we rarely get to the place of God's presence, we have missed what God has for us as His Church. We are not living His will, but our will. How can His presence be with us? How can we feed on Him? How can we receive His spiritual things and His gifts? How can we hear Him and see Him? His Church must get back to the place of the presence.

In His presence, we are fed and nourished to grow. It is in this place that we are dismantled and re-made by the Lord God and His Holy Spirit. The place of the presence is having a prayer life, fasting often, reading His word, meditating on His word, and fellowship. The Lord spoke to Moses when he was in His presence so he could pass it to the children of Israel. It has not changed today. We are the Priests of God and in order to know what the Spirit says to us, we need to always be close to Him.

When Lot was told to run to the Lord's presence, he argued and chose for himself a comfort zone where he felt it was good for him. Because God will not deny us the permissive will, He allowed him to go to the comfort zone, even though the secure place was the Lord's presence.

> *17As soon as they had brought them out, one of them said, "Flee for your lives! Don't look back, and don't stop anywhere in the plain! Flee to the mountains or you will be swept away!" 18But Lot said to them, "No, my lords, please! 19Your servant has found favor in you eyes, and you have shown*

> *great kindness to me in sparing my life. But I can't flee to the mountains; this disaster will overtake me, and I'll die. ²⁰Look, here is a town near enough to run to, and it is small. Let me flee to it—it is very small, isn't it? Then my life will be spared." ²¹He said to him, "Very well, I will grant this request too." - Genesis 19:17-21*

He ended up sleeping with his own daughters, bearing ungodly fruit. This is exactly what the Church of God is doing. She wants to dwell in the comfort zone where she feels everything is okay. She doesn't want to pay any sacrifice of going up the mountain. Many are bearing fruit that are not Godly. They have blessings that did not come from the Lord. They are in marriages that God did not approve. But they are in the Church. What kind of fruit are you bearing? Spiritual conception is done in God's presence, and so is Spiritual birthing.

If you conceive out of God's presence, you will surely give birth to fruit that God did not will for you. This is the reason the Lord wants us in His presence.

## *His Word*

> *The Word became flesh and dwelt among us, and we beheld His glory, the glory as of the only begotten of the Father, full of grace and truth. - John 1:14*

There is no doubt these are the last days, and those who understand this are completely engrossed in the Word of God. They are seeking to know the truth, being purified, being sanctified, and being cleansed. The Word of God is our truth that sanctifies and purifies us. The Church cannot run away from the Word. See these two Scriptures:

*Sanctify them by Your truth. Your Word is truth.*
*- John 17:17*

*Just as Christ LOVED the Church and gave Himself for her, to make her HOLY, CLEANSING her by the WASHING with water through the WORD. - Ephesians 5:25-26*

It is the Word that trains, corrects, and rebukes us (2 Timothy 3:16). All Scripture is God-breathed and is useful for teaching, rebuking, correcting, and training in righteousness.

It is the Word that operates, tests, tries, and exposes our sinful nature.

*For the Word of God is living and active. Sharper than any double-edged sword, it penetrates even to dividing soul and spirit, joints and marrow; it judges the thoughts and attitudes of the heart. [13]Nothing in all creation is hidden from God's sight. Everything is uncovered and laid bare before the eyes of Him to whom we must give account. - Hebrews 4:12-13*

The more we read the Word, the more we know God and His Word. The more we know the Word, the more revelation we gain. The more revelation we gain, the more truth we know. The more we know the truth, the more we are changed and transformed into Christ's likeness, and His glory is fully revealed in us.

The Word of God in us makes the difference. The end of everything is so near; the true Church is seeking nothing other than repentance, cleansing, sanctification, and purification.

The truth many do not want to hear is this: That holiness and righteousness is sought for. Yes, it is. The Lord said, "SEEK FIRST the KINGDOM of God and His RIGHTEOUSNESS" (Mathew 6:33). His word is our light, our truth, our food, and our life. The Church of Christ is empty and weak today because she has no Word. She is not being changed because she does not know the Word of God. She is not being filled by His Spirit because she has no understanding of the Word. She is not tapping into His blessings because she has no Word. She can't defeat the enemy if she has no Word. The Word is everything to His Church.

## *Seek His Face In Prayer*

*My heart says of you, "Seek His Face!" Your face, Lord, I will Seek. - Psalm 27:8*

Wise men sought for Him; Wise men still seek Him today. When the Wise-men heard about the birth of the Lord Jesus Christ, they sought Him, and when they found Him, they worshiped Him (Mathew 2:1-11). The Lord has commanded us to seek Him diligently. Only when we seek Him wholeheartedly shall we find Him (Jeremiah 29:13). Only those who seek Him, find Him.

While on earth, the Lord Jesus Christ spent His time in prayer and He is still interceding for His Church today. The Lord Jesus Christ knew that's where the power to do God's will is drawn. He was always at the secret place. Every time His disciples or others looked for Him, He was on the mountain praying (Mark 1:35-37). In the Garden of Gethsemane, He challenged His disciples to watch and pray instead of sleeping. He said to them, "Couldn't you men keep watch with Me for one hour?" (Mathew 26:40). He made them know that if they failed to pray, they would fall in temptation.

Time spent in prayer matters to His Church. It's through prayer that we draw power and strength to keep us going. How can His Church do without prayer? The Apostle Paul picks it up in his writings to encourage the

Church of Christ to pray continually (1 Thessalonian 5:17). One of the pieces of the armor of God in His scripture is prayer (Ephesians 6:18). The Church has been commanded to put on the full armor of God, so that she can be able to stand her ground when the day of evil comes. God's armor is His presence that shields His Church.

> *[13] Therefore, take up the full armor of God, so that you will be able to resist in the evil day, and having done everything, to stand firm. [14] Stand firm therefore, **having girded your loins with truth**, and **having put on the breastplate of righteousness**, [15] and having shod **your feet with the preparation of the gospel of peace**; [16] in addition to all, taking up the shield of faith with which you will be able to extinguish all the flaming arrows of the evil one. [17] And take **the helmet of salvation**, and the sword of the Spirit, which is the word of God. [18] With all prayer and petition pray at all times in the Spirit, and with this in view, be on the alert with all perseverance and petition for all the saints. - Ephesians 6:13-18*

Prayer is the Church's sword. The Church can never take her position overcoming the devil without this weapon. Today, His Church does not know the Lord because she never seeks Him in prayer. The altar of prayer is broken in His Church. She has forgotten the place of the presence. She is sleeping while she is supposed to keep watch in prayer. This is an altar that must be revived in His Church for His presence to return. It is through prayer that we connect and communicate with the Father. When the altar of prayer is alive in a Christian's life, she has the power to defeat the enemy. The reason the Church is falling into temptations and living in sin is because she has no prayer life. She lacks power to overcome sin. The Lord Jesus said to the disciples,

*Watch and pray so that you will not fall into temptation. The Spirit is willing, but the flesh is weak. - Mathew 26:41*

When the flesh is stronger than the spirit-man, he will rule by dictating a Christian's life. But when the spirit-man is stronger, he rules over the flesh. Paul was keen to warn the Church to live by the Spirit so that she would not fulfill the desires of the sinful nature (Galatians 5:16-17).

How can she live by the Spirit without prayer? It's through prayer that we build our personal relationship with the Father. It's through prayer that intimacy with the Father is developed. It's through prayer that deep love for the Lord is born. The closer we get, the closer we need Him to be to us. The closer He gets to His Church, the more His presence dwells within us. We need His presence with us. He is life to His Church. If she loses Him, she remains dead, even if she looks alive. The Church must restore the broken altar of prayer.

# Chapter 3
## *The Press and the Fire*

*<sup>14</sup>But thanks be to God, who always leads us as captives in Christ's triumphal procession and uses us to spread the aroma of the knowledge of Him everywhere. <sup>15</sup>For we are to God the pleasing aroma of Christ among those who are being saved and those who are perishing. <sup>16</sup>To the one we are an aroma that brings death; to the other, an aroma that brings life. And who is equal to such a task? - 2 Corinthians 2:14-16*

Even after the sanctuary has been built, it is not over yet. The fire awaits. The Lord is coming for a Church with neither wrinkle nor spot. Don't run away from the threshing floor. Don't run away from the press. Don't run away from the fire. His Church needs all of these to be complete. We must be tried, tested, and approved by God.

So much has got to die so that the Spirit of God can take total control. The Lord Himself makes us. For He is the Refiner's fire. But He can't do it unless we surrender. We must submit to the test. Once we surrender to Him, we are no longer seen in our sinful nature, but we are seen as His perfect bride.

> *²But who can endure the day of His coming? And who can stand when He appears? For He is like a refiner's fire, and like launderers' soap. ³He will sit as a refiner and a purifier of silver; He will purify the sons of Levi, and purge them as gold and silver, that they may offer to the LORD an offering in righteousness. - Malachi 3:2-3*

> *This third I will put into the fire; I will refine them like silver and test them like gold. They will call on My name and I will answer them; I will say, "They are my people," and they will say, "The LORD is our God." - Zechariah 13:9*

When the Lord Jesus Christ is commanding us to take up our cross daily and to follow Him, He Himself is carrying a sword (His Word) to operate on us and fire (His Spirit) to purify us. This is accomplished in His presence. God chose a specific place for Isaac to be offered as a sacrifice. Mount Moriah was God's presence (Genesis 22:14). We see Isaac carrying the wood which signifies his cross, while Abraham, his father, carries the knife which signifies the sword of the Spirit, and the fire which signifies the Holy Spirit.

When they come to the chosen place, Isaac is bound and tied. He does not fight back nor resist, meaning he has totally surrendered. He has said yes to the will of his father, however painful it is.

It is the Word of God that operates on us, tests us, and tries us as the Spirit of God transforms us.

> *$^{12}$For the Word of God is alive and active. Sharper than any double-edged sword, it penetrates even to dividing soul and spirit, joints and marrow; it judges the thoughts and attitudes of the heart. $^{13}$Nothing in all creation is hidden from God's sight. Everything is uncovered and laid bare before the eyes of him to whom we must give account. - Hebrews 4:12-13*

> *$^{16}$All scripture is God-breathed and is useful for teaching, rebuking, correcting and training in Righteousness, $^{17}$so that the man of God may be thoroughly equipped for every good work. - 2 Timothy 3:16-17*

We have been created to be a fragrance of the Lord Jesus Christ unto Father God. But! There is a triumphal procession we must undergo (2 Corinthians 2:14-15). No one can triumph in the Flesh; It must be by the SPIRIT. The truth is: it's only *pressed* petals that give the pure perfume. It's only *pressed* olives that give the pure anointing oil. It's only *pressed* grapes that give the pure wine.

The Lord Jesus Christ broke His body on the cross to save the world. By pouring out His life, heaven and earth were filled with the fragrance of His life. This is the same aroma the remnant Church must manifest. It only happens when the life and person of Christ is worked into our lives through the Holy Spirit. This leads to transformation in Christ's likeness by the Spirit of God (2 Corinthians 3:18).

Do we all agree that there is a crushing process? Yes! The flesh (our sinful nature) must die for the Spirit to live.

Our pure fragrance to Father God, and to the nations, is living in prayer, living in true worship, living in repentance, and bearing the fruit of the Spirit - which is love. None of these can be accomplished in the flesh. The flesh must die.

We are grains of wheat, and unless we fall on the ground to die, we will never produce (John 12:24). This can only be accomplished in a sanctified and Spirit-filled life. The Lord says to His Church today:

> *Can I not do with you as the potter does to the clay? For like clay in the potter's hand, so are you in My hand. - Jeremiah 18:6*

If the Church has been freely called by the Lord to gain access into the Holy of Holies, why has she denied herself the best part? Why is the larger part of the Church still lodging at the outer court? Why is it that a very small part of the Church has managed to press through into the Holy of Holies, while the rest are okay residing outside? She must be running away from a process that can only be accomplished at the altar of incense, which was placed in between the Holy Place and the Holy of Holies. It is on this altar that the life and person of Christ Jesus is worked in us through the Holy Spirit. There must be death to self and self-will for us to become the fragrance of God. It's all about manifesting His fragrance; for we are the aroma of Christ.

It's not until we allow the Ark of the Covenant, who is the Lord Jesus Christ and His presence, to be formed in us, as we walk daily in Him, learning obedience to the Father, that we can be carriers of His manifest presence. A vessel that is not living in God's will cannot carry and manifest His glory. This means this vessel has not died to self and self-will. She is living in pride. Humility has not been attained by her. She still wants to do things her way, pursue her self-will, and embrace her plans.

Only when this process is accomplished in a believer's life will he/she begin to manifest the fragrance of the Lord. When she is completely dead to self, the Spirit takes over, and therefore she can be able to access the most holy place.

Flesh cannot survive in this place. It is our living flesh that has hindered us from getting into God's depths. The reason we have been commanded to carry the cross daily is to put the flesh to death. The cross is a place of crucifixion. His Church must die daily for Christ to live in her (2 Corinthians 4:10).

# Chapter 4
## *His Holy Spirit*

*$^{28}$And it shall come to pass afterward, that I will pour out my Spirit on all flesh; your sons and your daughters shall prophesy, your old men shall dream dreams, and your young men shall see visions. $^{29}$Even on the male and female servants in those days I will pour out my Spirit. $^{30}$And I will show wonders in the heavens and on the earth, blood and fire and columns of smoke. - Joel 2:28*

The Ark of the Covenant is a symbol of the Holy Spirit. He gave the Israelites directions on when to move, when to camp, where to move, and how to move while in the wilderness (Exodus 40:36-38), (Numbers 9: 15-23). It is the Spirit of God that leads His Church to all truth. The Church of God cannot do without the power of the Holy Spirit. The Lord Jesus Christ told His disciples to wait in Jerusalem for the power of the Holy Spirit before they went out to witness about Him (Acts 1:4,8). The Gospel and the Holy Spirit are inseparable. We cannot witness the Lord without His Holy Spirit. It is He that helps and guides the Church into all truth (John 16:7-12). It is He that leads His Church to the right path (Isaiah 30:21). It is He that helps us in our weaknesses, by interceding for us in groans that words cannot express, in accordance with God's will (Romans 8:26). It is He that reveals to us the secret things of God. We must receive Him through baptism.

When believers receive salvation, there is a measure of the Holy Spirit deposited in them. This is not enough. We need Holy Spirit baptism. It is after this experience that a believer begins to grow spiritually from level to level as they are filled by the Holy Spirit continually. The Church of Christ needs to be filled to overflowing. Without the Holy Spirit, no Christian can grow in the Lord.

When Ezekiel was led through the water, he realized that after each measure, the waters rose to a higher level.

> *³And when the man that had the line in his hand went forth eastward, he measured a thousand cubits, and he brought me through the waters; the waters were to the ankles. ⁴Again he measured a thousand, and brought me through the waters; the waters were to the knees. Again, he measured a thousand, and brought me through; the waters were to the loins. ⁵Afterward he measured a thousand; and it was a river that I could not pass over: for the waters were risen, waters to swim in, a river that could not be passed over. - Ezekiel 47:3-5*

He grew to the fullness of the Spirit, where the waters were a river that one could not cross over, but he had to swim. There is a deeper place the Lord is calling His Church to. When we get to this level, the Spirit takes full control of us. This is the time we surrender and yield to His leading because He bears us up. We fully depend on Him. The more He fills us, the more we need Him. We can never be full of Him because we grow in Him daily. He begins to work in us. It is His Spirit that transforms us into the likeness of the Lord Jesus Christ (2 Corinthians 3:18). It is through Him that God dwells within us (1 Corinthians 3:16). It is by His Spirit that we receive spiritual things from the Father.

> *The person without the Spirit does not accept the things that come from the Spirit of God but considers them foolishness, and cannot understand them because they are discerned only through the Spirit. - 1 Corinthians 2:14*

It is by His Spirit that God reveals to us what He has prepared for us (1 Corinthians 2:9-10). It is by the Holy Spirit we hear the voice of God, the will of God, and the plan of God. It is by the Spirit of God that we receive power to serve the Lord effectively (Acts 1:8) and by this power that the Church overcomes temptation, and withstands trials and tests. It is by this power that we destroy the works of Satan (Luke 10:19).

By His Spirit we can walk in boldness, without fear. By the Spirit we can see our sin and receive our forgiveness. He warns us when we sin and He leads us into repentance. The closer we are with the Holy Spirit, the more aware we are of our disobedience to God. He is Holy, and will always lead us in His Holiness, without which no one shall see the Lord. There is a level of Holy-Spirit-fullness that the Lord wants His Church to be filled with.

The seven Spirits of the Lord are key to His Church (Isaiah 11:1-2):

1. The Spirit of the Lord
2. The Spirit of Wisdom
3. The Spirit of Understanding
4. The Spirit of Counsel
5. The Spirit of Might
6. The Spirit of Knowledge
7. The fear of the Lord

With all these, His Church has the fullness of the Lord Jesus Christ.

Today, a bigger part of the Body of Christ does not know the Holy Spirit. She has no relationship with Him. She has received only the smaller measure of His Spirit at salvation and remains at this limit. She was baptized in the Holy Spirit, but still operates with the ankle-level measure. She has no idea what being filled by the Holy Spirit is and has no idea what thirsting for the Spirit of

God is. Because of this, the manifestation of Gifts of the Spirit are not in His Church. It is He, the Holy Spirit that gives these gifts to the Church as He wills. She has no revelation of the Word of God. A Christian will go nowhere without revelation. The only way to know God is by revelation.

There are so few miracles in the Church of Christ because the power of the Holy Spirit is not in the Church. She is walking in sin because she is not dead to flesh. She seeks to fulfill the desires of the sinful nature because her spirit-man is weak.

She is full of herself, and she doesn't hunger and thirst for His Spirit. She is drawing water from cisterns that cannot sustain her (Jeremiah 2:13). The Lord Jesus said to the Samaritan woman who had come to draw water from the well she was familiar with according to her religion,

> *Everyone who drinks this water will thirst again, but whoever drinks the water I give him will never thirst. Indeed, the water I give him will become in him a spring of water welling up to eternal life.*
> *- John 4:13-14*

The Lord Jesus Christ helped us know how important His Spirit is to His Church. The Spirit is the key. Scripture says,

> *In the last day, that great day of the feast, Jesus stood and cried, saying, if any man thirsts, let him come unto me, and drink. - John 7:37*

At feasts people drink the best drinks, eat the most delicious meals, and celebrate with friends and relatives. The event is filled with joy and delight. Jesus knew these people needed more than what solely satisfied the flesh at the feast. They needed the Holy Spirit. That's why He distinctly said that we should thirst and drink from what *He* gives.

Where will the Lord and His presence dwell if His Spirit is not with His Church? Where will the Presence of the Lord dwell if His temple is not made by His Spirit? It's time the Church began to desire not only to be baptized by the Holy Spirit, but to be filled daily by His Spirit. We must be filled to overflowing in order to be fruitful (Ezekiel 47: 7-12). The Lord said to Ezekiel:

> *This water flows towards the eastern region, goes down into the valley, and enters the sea. When it reaches the sea, its waters are healed. Every living thing that moves, wherever the river go, will live. Along the bank of the river, shall grow all kinds of trees used for food. Their leaves will not wither, and their fruit will not fail. Their fruit will be for food and their leaves for healing. - Ezekiel 47:8-12*

The deeper we get, the more fruitful we become as we release spiritual food and healing to the nations. We must be filled by His Spirit in order to grow into His holiness, because the Spirit transforms us by filtering away what is *not* of God, and filling us with what *is* of God. The Lord is calling His Church to be filled with the fullness of His Spirit (Isaiah 11:2).

The Seven-fold Ministry of God are the eyes of the Spirit.

> *The Spirit of the Lord will rest on Him, the Spirit of Wisdom and Understanding, the Spirit of Counsel and of Power, the Spirit of Knowledge and of the fear of the Lord. And He will delight in the fear of the Lord. - Isaiah 11:2-3*

When the Church achieves this fullness of His Spirit, the Lord Himself is fully formed in her. She reflects nothing other than the presence of God, the glory of God, the likeness of God, and the nature of God. This is where the Lord wants His Church to be. The Lord is calling us to come to Him and drink of His waters (Isaiah 55:1-2). The Spirit is freely given to His Church without cost. Many are spending money to buy things that cannot quench their spiritual thirst. And because the spiritual thirst is not quenched within the Church, she is empty and a void remains. If the Holy Spirit does not occupy the Church, then we can never live a holy life. It is He, the Spirit that helps us by changing us and making us holy vessels. When holiness abounds, God and His presence have a dwelling place.

# Chapter 5
## *Holiness of God*

*Since we have these promises, dear friends, let us purify ourselves from everything that contaminates body and spirit, perfecting HOLINESS out of reverence for God. - 2 Corinthians 7:1*

God is holy and therefore, His sons and daughters must be holy (1 Peter 1:16). The Ark of the Covenant was placed in the Holy of Holies. The Holy of Holies was a place not everyone entered, including the priests. Only the *High Priest* was allowed to enter the Holy of Holies, and he could only enter once a year. Before he entered, he was to sanctify himself to be made holy. This speaks greatly on how the Church of Christ needs holiness to gain access to His holy courts and to meet with the Holy God. Holiness is to be sought after. Scripture says,

*Make every effort to live in peace with everyone and to be holy; without holiness, no one will see the Lord. - Hebrews 12:14*

Becoming holy is a process one attains by living in repentance. The Levites who served at the altar were to be holy in every way. We, as the Church, are the priests today, and such holiness is required of us too. The Lord told Moses to prepare the Levites in a special way before they served Him. They were to be holy to God because He, the Lord, is holy. (Leviticus 20: 26). 1 Chronicles 15:12-15 describes David's exhortation for the priests to "consecrate themselves" in preparation for carrying the Ark of God. This tells us how holy the Lord wants us to be if we are to serve Him, approach Him, and enter His courts.

The Church of Christ is a peculiar people, set apart by God for Himself. Preparing ourselves through sanctification means to be made holy, or set apart, for a divine purpose. As New Testament priests, we must allow God to cleanse us so that His glory will shine in our lives. The Lord is coming for a holy Church with neither wrinkle nor spot. Today the presence of God has departed from His Church because she is defiled, she is not living in repentance. She does not have the fear of the Lord in her. She lives as she wants. She is not seeking holiness. God is holy and His presence will only dwell in a holy vessel.

God was always concerned about cleanliness in the camp. The Israelites were to keep the camp clean for the Lord to be closer to them.

*For the Lord your God moves about in your camp to protect you and to deliver your enemies to you. Your camp must be holy, so that He will not see among you anything indecent and turn away from you. - Deuteronomy 23:14*

Every time the Children of Israel were to go and meet with the Lord, they were to take a three-day preparation (Exodus 19:10-11). If holiness is key for the Church to meet with the Lord, then we need holiness. The Church of Christ must come back to seeking holiness and righteousness. The veil was torn from top to bottom, meaning, we have free access to the Holy of Holies. But no one will enter the Holy of Holies without first being sanctified, cleansed, and purified.

The Ark of the Covenant was placed in the Holy of Holies and just above it -- between the Cherubim. The Lord said He would meet and speak with Moses (Exodus 25:22). How will she, the Church, meet and speak with the Lord if she does not enter the Holy of Holies? How will she enter the Holy of Holies if she does not keep clean? If the Ark of the Covenant dwelled in the most holy place, the Church needs to be holy for the Ark of the Covenant to be formed within her. Samuel the Prophet, was set apart for the Lord as a holy and living sacrifice by his mother, Hannah (1 Samuel 1:11). We see this fulfilled in 1 Samuel 1:28. Hannah brought her son, Samuel, to the temple and gave him over to God.

> *So now I give him to the Lord. For his whole life,*
> *he shall be given over to the Lord. - 1 Samuel 1:28*

It is clear when we see him lying in the temple next to the Ark of the Covenant and the Lord gives him a special assignment. These are the days when the voice of God was rare and there were no visions (1 Samuel 3:1). The Church must press herself into the Holy of Holies to meet and speak with the Lord. But she must remain holy, for the Lord is holy. The basin of washing was placed right before the holy place. The reason was for the priests to put away uncleanliness before they entered the Holy of Holies. It is not different today. We need holiness to access the Holy of Holies. We must die to self, a process that will call us to be crushed on the alter of incense, before we get in the Holy of Holies. This is what the Lord commands the Church to seek. His Church needs holiness and the Lord wants holiness from her. When His fullness is formed within us, our Spirit-man becomes the Holy of Holies. With this, we reflect nothing but Christ Jesus the Lord. We can now access the most holy place. It is when she enters His holy presence that she meets and speaks with the Lord personally. She personally knows her God and God knows her by name. She speaks the very words of the Lord and thus she becomes like Him. She develops a personal relationship with the Father that develops into deep love and intimacy. At this level, she cannot do without Him.

# Chapter 6

## *His Deep Love*

*He has taken me to the banquet hall, and His banner over me is Love. - Songs of Solomon 2:4*

There is no other LOVE than experiencing the Lord's love as our Bridegroom. Many people have heard of the love of the Lord, but have never fully tasted this love. Many speak about the love of the Lord, but they have no idea of what this love is. This is because the Church hasn't arrived at the place the Lord is calling her.

The Lord told Hosea that He was going to allure His people to a chosen place, and speak tenderly to them (Hosea 2:14). It was after winning her heart at this place that the Lord said He would betroth her to Him in love.

*I will betroth you to me forever: I will betroth you in righteousness and justice, in love and compassion. I will betroth you in faithfulness and you will acknowledge the Lord. - Hosea 2: 19-20*

Has the Lord taken you to the banquet hall? Is His banner over you, love? (Songs of Solomon 2:4). This is a place you don't want to miss. A place you never want to ever leave. He must become yours, and you must become His. (Songs of Solomon 2:16). Has the Lord stolen your heart? (Songs of Solomon 4:9). You must hold tight to Him and never let Him go (Songs of Solomon 3:4b). This is the love we are talking about. There is a depth in the Lord you need to get to. Paul encourages the Church to be rooted and grounded in love.

> *That Christ may **dwell** in your hearts through **faith**; that you, being **rooted** and **grounded** in **love**, may be able to **comprehend** what is the **width** and **length** and **depth** and **height** of His **love**; to **know** the **love** of God which Passes **knowledge**. - Ephesians 3:17-18*

*God is love. - 1 John 4:16*

His love for His Church is indescribable, but His Church cannot experience this amazing love until she fully gives herself to Him. Two people who are in love reciprocate their feelings for each other. The Lord loves His Church, but because His Church does not love Him back with her whole heart, mind, and soul she can't experience, taste, feel, touch, and smell His pure love. Until we make Him our Lord, we can't love Him as He desires.

Mary Magdalene graduated her love for the Lord Jesus Christ at the tomb. When she went to call the disciples, she referred to Him as the Lord (John 20:2), but later, after the disciples went back to their homes, she began to seek Him diligently, in deep worship. The more she dwelt in His presence, the more she personalized the Lord and called Him, "My Lord" (John 20: 13). It is this love that made her linger in the Lord's presence until she saw Him with her own eyes. This is the love the Lord desires His Church to have for Him. The measure of love you have for the Lord will plant you in His depths - the realms where you will experience His deep love.

It is this love that will dare you to go past the watchmen in the night and to seek for the One you love (Songs of Solomon 3:4). It is this love that will make you grab hold of the Lord and never to let Him go (Songs of Solomon 3:4). When this love for the Lord deepens, you can't do without Him. His presence becomes a priority. You want to meet with Him, see Him, hear Him, and speak with Him every moment. You begin to look like Him. The fruit of the Spirit, which is love, develops and flows in you to Him and to the souls around you. Where love is, His presence abides. The Lord has commanded us to love Him and our neighbours.

> *Jesus replied, "Love the Lord your God with all your heart and with all your soul and with all your mind. This is the first and greatest com-*

> *mandment. And the second is like it: Love your neighbor as yourself." - Mathew 22:37-39*

Is this love in the Church of Christ today? Not yet. How did the early church demonstrate God's love? They were all equal before God. They sold all of their belongings and shared them equally amongst them -- the poor were not left out. They forsook all else to follow Jesus Christ - this world was not their home. They discovered a city built not with human hands, but by the instruction of God. They started the journey to the Holy of Holies. That's why it's written, "He who has the love of the world, the love of the Father is not in him." (1 John 2:15)

Today, the Church loves the Lord with their lips, but not their hearts. There is no love for one another. The Church of Christ chooses whom to give love to. The Church of Christ lives in gossip, jealousy, hatred, unforgiveness, selfishness, pride, bitterness, anger, and so on because she has no love for one another. She has developed a love for worldly things more than a love for Christ. The devil is using her against one another because she has not allowed God to use her to love and support one another. She is devouring and destroying others (Galatians 5:15). This has killed the presence of the Lord in His Church. His likeness is not in His Church. Where is the love of the Lord in His Church? This is not the heart of the Lord. We must allow the fruit of the Spirit, which is love, to develop within us (Galatians 5:22). This is the **true** likeness of Christ the Lord.

His Church must develop a personal intimate relationship with the Lord God if she wants to spend eternity with Him. She must begin to love Him now. Love is a process that graduates from one level to the other. Faithfulness, commitment, and trust builds it. The more we know each other, the deeper the love gets until we can't let go of one another. Yes! The presence of each other is key here.

*And now these three remain: Faith, hope and love. But the greatest of these is love. - 1 Corinthians 13:13*

When love deepens, the lovers become intimate. You can only become intimate with the lover of your heart. It can never be otherwise.

## *Intimacy with God*

*[14] Therefore I am going to allure her; I will lead her into the desert and speak tenderly to her... [16] "In that day," declares the Lord, "You will call me 'my husband'; you will no longer call me, 'my master.'" - Hosea 2:14, 16*

Intimacy with God begins when the love deepens and we radically pursue Him with our whole hearts. This is why we can't do without Him. We want to be in His presence more than anywhere else. Seeking His face becomes the only choice we have. King David wrote,

*When You said, "Seek My face," my heart said to You, "Your face, O Lord, I shall seek." - Psalm 27:8*

God invites us to draw near to Him and He will draw near to us (James 4:8). Bible reading and prayer is not enough. We must take time alone with Him, asking for nothing but more of Him -- More of His fullness and more of His presence in our everyday lives.

No one can become who they have not seen. The reason the Church today is not reflecting Christ is because she is far away from Him. She does not personally know Him, but only hears about him. She has not denied her flesh so she may fully follow Him as He commanded us. It is only the Christians who choose to follow Jesus daily that are transformed into His LIKENESS by the Holy Spirit. The more we dwell in his presence, the more He fills us and the more we become like Him.

Until we see Him, and establish a close relationship of love and intimacy with Him, we can never know Him. Unless we know Him, we can never become like Him. You become what you behold (John 1:14). When Moses asked to see God's GLORY, the Lord said to him: "There is a place near Me where you may stand on a rock" (Exodus 33:21). Draw closer to Him. Become like Him.

God releases power through us as we dwell in intimacy with Him. If this is not yet your deepest desire, then the other "loves" in your life must be thrown away. You can't have intimacy with the Lord without having made Him the love of your life. The Lord can't be the love of your life when He hasn't possessed your heart. The Lord is asking us to give Him our whole hearts (Proverbs 23:26). All He wants is our hearts. You must become His, and He must become yours (Songs of Solomon 2:16).

Joshua knew that for the people to yield their hearts to the Lord, they needed to get rid of other gods (Joshua 24:23). The Church must have a deep desire for profound intimacy with the Lord Jesus Christ -- to personally know Him (John 17:3), bear much fruit (John 15:8), and to see Him and His glory (John 20:14, John 1:14).

The Lord God has called us to have intimacy with Him, but earthly temptations have separated us from this special union.

Reflecting on what the Lord Jesus said to the two sisters, we see that Martha was distracted by the preparation that had to be made, while Mary sat at the Lord's feet listening to what He said (Luke 10:39-42). The Lord said, "Martha, Martha you are distracted by so many things. But only ONE thing is needed. Mary has chosen what is better, and it will not be taken away from her" [Intimacy]. It's about *knowing* the Lord, not just knowing *about* the Lord.

Intimacy with the Lord Jesus Christ keeps you in the Spirit. If the relationship is to last forever, we need to live in the Spirit, for the Lord God is Spirit (John 4:23). Flesh cannot relate with the Spirit. The Spirit only relates with the Spirit.

You must be changed into a new (born again) person in order to fully relate with Him. The more the love deepens, the more we become like Him because He fills us to His fullness.

When you leave the Spirit realm the closeness diminishes. It becomes hard for you to hear Him, see Him, touch Him, smell Him, feel Him, and taste of Him. The relationship weakens because there is no more communion with Him nor any more love for Him. It's hard for you to think about Him and speak of Him frequently. You begin to feel emptiness and dryness. His spiritual things become valueless and meaningless. You begin to struggle to be in His presence. You begin to seek His hand but not His face. Yet when you keep in the Spirit, the closeness deepens. The bond of relationship grows stronger and you find that you can't do without Him. You begin to hunger and thirst for Him, for He is all you need. You begin to search for Him every single moment. The only place you want to be is in His presence. Hearing Him, seeing Him, feeling Him, touching Him, smelling Him, and tasting of Him becomes a lifestyle. You begin to think about Him and speak about Him always. Then, He begins to reveal secrets and utter mysteries to your ears. Nothing is hidden from you. His joy and peace fill your heart, because you are in love. You begin to have access to the riches of His glory. He begins to satisfy you with good things. He becomes yours and you become His and you begin to seek His face, not His hand, because all you need is Him. This is the very place the Lord God is calling His very own.

What the church has failed to do is to fully give herself to the Lord. She does not know God personally, she only knows greatly about Him. She cannot receive His blessings, because her Love for Him has not developed into intimacy. How will she be made into what God wants? How will she be designed into a vessel that can carry and reflect the glory of the Lord God? She must come back to the place of intimacy and her relationship with God must develop into love and intimacy. It is this bond of love that will keep the presence of God within, upon, and around the Church. When we personally know Him, we understand His worth. We can't just give Him any little thing. We give Him what He deserves. He deserves true worship. He deserves pure and holy sacrifices. Our lives are changed into living and holy sacrifices because all we seek is to please Him as the Lover of our souls.

# Chapter 7
## *Worship*

*Therefore, I urge you brothers in view of God's mercy to offer your bodies as living sacrifices, holy and pleasing to God, for this is your spiritual act of worship. - Romans 12:1*

God invites us to draw near to Him and He will draw near to us (James 4:8). Bible reading and prayer is not enough. We must take time alone with Him, only asking for more of Him -- more of His fullness and more of His presence in our everyday lives.

Worship must be a lifestyle. It is not limited to a specific place, time, or day. The four living creatures and the twenty-four elders worship God day and night without resting (Revelation 4:8-11). His Church is not an exception. From the beginning, the Lord created us to worship Him. The main reason the Israelites were delivered from Egypt was to worship God (Exodus 4:23). Worship is a spiritual act that allows us to spiritually connect with the Father. It must be a living sacrifice. It is done in truth and in Spirit (John 4:23-24). God is Spirit, and worship must be spiritually driven. The Samaritan woman religiously followed the traditions of worship of her fathers and Jesus rebuked her belief (John 4:20-22). We can never worship God in religious rules or tradition. We must come back to the true heart of worship.

The true presence of God that goes with praise and worship is not there today. Scripture says the Lord God inhabits the praises of His people (Psalm 22:3). If the Lord is to be in our midst, then we must offer holy and genuine sacrifices of worship.

Since God is holy, holiness is key. But why is the church of God giving the Lord defiled sacrifices instead of worship? Why is she lifting defiled hands to the Lord? Until we come to an understanding that worship is a lifestyle, a spiritual act, and a living sacrifice (Romans 12:1), we will religiously give Him defiled and unacceptable worship with our lips. And this is what the Church is doing today: She does not know her God, and so she does not know what He deserves and gives Him anything in the name of worship. She must seek holiness and righteousness and embrace sanctification and purification before she worships.

When David was bringing back the Ark of the Covenant to Jerusalem, he danced with all his might, and everyone with him celebrated with shouts and the sound of trumpets (2 Samuel 6:14-15). When his wife, Michal, despised him, David rebuked her. He said to her,

> *It was before the Lord, who chose me rather than your father or anyone from his house when He appointed me ruler over Israel. I will celebrate before the Lord. I will become even more undignified than this, and I will be humiliated in my own eyes. - 2 Samuel 6:21-22*

This is how the Church should praise and worship the Father. She needs to get lost in the Spirit without thinking about who is next to her or what they will say. It's a spiritual act and flesh should not be glorified by it. Why is her heart far away as her lips proclaim worship?

The Lord God says,

> *These people honor Me with their lips but their hearts are far from Me. They worship Me in vain. - Mathew 15:8-9*

Our hearts must be sincere to the Lord God. If the presence of God is to be in our midst, then we must be broken, and have a contrite spirit. The spirit of humility must be embraced. The devil uses the spirit of pride to kill the presence of God. The Church is operating in the flesh more than the Spirit.

The Church has not died to self. She has not broken the alabaster jar (Mark 14:3). She is holding on it, but claiming to worship the Lord. If the oil in the alabaster jar is not flowing yet, then the fragrance is not filling the room. When the wise men came to see Jesus soon after His birth, they worshiped Him with treasures of gold, incense, and myrrh (Mathew 2:11). Even today, we must worship the Lord with the same treasures.

- Gold: Righteous vessels that have been refined and purified by the Refiner's fire (Malachi 3:3).

- Incense: Life, and person, of Christ should be working in us through the Holy Spirit (2 Corinthians 3:18). There must be death to self and self-will.

- Myrrh: The Fragrance and aroma of Christ (Corinthians 2:14). Until we realize that the true worship the Father seeks is a spiritual act, and every sacrifice we give unto Him is spiritual, we will remain religious in our worship to God by our physical acts and words.

Scripture says:

*The sacrifices of God are a broken spirit; a broken and a contrite heart, O God, you will not despise.*
*- Psalm 51:17*

It is through this true spiritual worship that God's presence is made manifest. He comes down to deliver His people, heal His people, bless His people, and commune with His people. His presence fills the Church.

# Chapter 8
## *God's Manifest Presence*

*The Lord replied, "My Presence will go with you, and I will give you rest." - Exodus 33:14*

Christians are meant to live in God's presence, move in God's presence, and to manifest God's presence. When the presence departs, the believer loses the most expensive and important gift the world can ever have. The presence of the Lord should matter more in a Christian's life than anything else on earth. When the Lord first created man, He placed him in His garden, which was His presence (Genesis 2:15). It is God's will and plan that His Church should live in His presence.

Why is it key for the Church of Christ to have His presence within her, upon her, and around her? It is because His presence distinguishes us. The only thing that makes the difference in a Christian's life is the Lord's presence. We have been specifically created as vessels of honour, to reflect His manifest glory on earth.

Moses saw the need for God's presence above everything else. He knew well that the land of Canaan was blessed, flowing with milk and honey. The Israelites had been told by God that they would live in houses they did not build, and eat foods they did not plant. But Moses still told the Lord that they couldn't go without His presence. Moses was not ready to go and possess the goodies of the land without the presence of God.

> *Then Moses said to him, "If your presence does not go with us, do not send us up from here." - Exodus 33:15*

How can the Body of Christ be distinguished from the world today if she loses the Lord's presence? The Lord's presence distinguishes the lives of Christians from other people on the face of the earth. Moses was concerned about going without God's presence. He knew there would be no distinction between them and the other people on the face of the earth. He said to the Lord,

> *How will anyone know that you are pleased with me and with your people unless You go with us? What else will distinguish me and Your people from all the other people on the face of the earth? - Exodus 33:16*

It was when Moses dwelt in God's presence that the Lord's Glory manifested through him.

> *²⁹When Moses came down from Mount Sinai with the two tablets of the covenant law in his hands, he was not aware that his face was radiant because he had spoken with the LORD. ³⁰When Aaron and all the Israelites saw Moses, his face was radiant, and they were afraid to come near him. - Exodus 34:29-30*

Today the Church of Christ goes without the Lord's presence. She doesn't know and understand the preciousness of the Lord's presence in her life. She would rather possess material things than the presence of God. The Church of Christ must dwell in His presence. When we dwell in His presence we begin to live it. His Glory must shine upon His Church. The only thing the Church should be seeking is God's Presence.

How can she do without it? It's His presence that gives us identity as sons and daughters of His Kingdom. David said,

> *One thing I **ask** of the Lord, this is what I **seek**: That I may **dwell** in the House of the Lord All the Days of my **life**, to **gaze** upon the **beauty** of the Lord and to **seek** Him in His Temple. - Psalm 27:4*

If His glory is to be revealed to the earth (Romans 8:19), there must be surrendered sons of God seeking and living in Holiness, to manifest this glory (2 Corinthians 2:14-15). The sword of the Spirit must be at work in us daily (Hebrews 4:12-13).

It's when His Word, who is Christ the Lord, who is the **HOLY SPIRIT**, who is God Himself, finds His dwelling in us that we begin to manifest His Glory (John 1:14).

Glory doesn't come easily to a person. Crushing must take place first. That's why we need to take up the cross daily (Luke 9:23). God desires us to be crushed into powder and re-moulded again in His exact shape (Exodus 25:9).

Yes! Until the Ark of the Covenant, which is God's glory, who is God's presence, who is Christ's likeness, is formed in us, we can't carry and manifest His glory. It was when the Ark of the Covenant had been placed into the inner sanctuary of the temple, the most holy place, that the cloud filled the house of the Lord so the priests could not continue ministering because of the cloud; for the **GLORY** of the Lord filled the House of the Lord (1 Kings 8:10-11).

The glory doesn't just come upon everyone titled "Christian". Remember, many are called but few are chosen (Mathew 22:14). The Lord Jesus Christ said that anyone who wishes to come after Him must deny himself, take up his cross daily, and follow Him (Luke 9:23). This is not a cheap action. Many have taken up the cross, but are not willing to be crucified on that very cross for

Christ's sake. Many have taken up the cross, but they are not willing to follow Him. Many have answered the call, but they have not fully surrendered to the Master's will. There must be crushing before the glory manifests.

Key persons in scripture, such as Joseph, Moses, David, Ruth, Hannah, Jacob, Paul, John the Baptist, and the Lord Jesus Christ went through this. His Church is not an exception. It's not about Christian titles; it's about transformation into Christ's likeness through breaking, crushing, pressing, then making, moulding and shaping. It's only after this process that we, as vessels, can reflect His manifest glory. We must choose to seek His presence. Those who understand the preciousness of His presence cannot go without His presence. It is because His presence is life.

Those living this reality know that nothing and nothing on this earth can compare.

His presence within us means we have His exceedingly great power to do His will, overcome the enemy, overcome trials and tests, overcome temptations, and serve Him. His manifest presence within the Church means His fullness within the Church.

# Chapter 9
## *Power of God*

*And His incomparably great power for us who believe. That power is the same as the mighty strength. - Ephesians 1:19*

The Kingdom is power and authority. The "Ark of the Covenant" is the power and authority. Without it we are mere servants. The Ark originally provided safety to the Israelites in their journey to the Promised Land. The power of the Ark was manifested several times and enemies were scattered and destroyed. With the presence of the Ark, the waters of the River Jordan divided so the Israelites could cross on dry land (Joshua 3:14-17). With the presence of the Ark, the walls of Jericho fell so that the Israelites could capture the city (Joshua 6:6-21).

It is by His power that the Israelites were delivered from Egypt. Today, the power of God should be with His Church. Without His power, the Church is reduced to nothing. In the book of Acts, the Lord told the disciples to wait upon the promised gift before they left Jerusalem.

> *But you will receive power when the Holy Spirit comes on you; and you will be My witnesses in Jerusalem, and in all Judea, and Samaria and to the end of the earth. - Acts 1:8*

No Christian can do without the incomparable power of God. It is His power in us that enables us to serve Him, to stand strong, to overcome, and to do mighty things in His name. It's key for the Church of Christ to possess His power. The reason the Church of Christ is not serving God effectively is because she has lost the power of God that has been freely given to her. How will she overcome the enemy without the mighty power of God?

> *Behold, I give unto you power to tread on serpents and scorpions, and over all the power of the enemy: and nothing shall by any means hurt you. - Luke 10:19*

When the Israelites went to war with the Philistines without the Ark of the Covenant, they were defeated (1 Samuel 4:3). The power in the Ark of the Covenant during the old times is the same power the Church of Christ can't do without today. She must bring back the Ark of the Covenant which is God's power. How will the Church of Christ walk in miracles and wonders? The Lord Jesus Christ said those who believe in Him would do greater things than what He did (John 14:12). But is this promise being fulfilled? When the woman with the issue of blood touched the Lord Jesus Christ, she received her healing immediately.

The beauty of this is the Lord Jesus Christ realized that power had gone out of Him (Mark 5:30). The power of God was present for Him to heal the sick when the paralytic man on the mat was brought before the Lord (Luke 5:17). Miracles can only happen when His power is present.

Overcoming trials and tests is a process no Christian can run away from. But can she do this without the power of God in Her?

> *But we have this treasure in jars of clay to show that this all-surpassing power is from God and not from us. We are hard pressed on every side, but not crushed: perplexed, but not in despair: persecuted, but not abandoned: struck down, but not destroyed. - 2 Corinthians 4:7-9*

God's presence is our power and our weapon of warfare. When the Ark of the Covenant was taken by the Philistines to the house of Dagon and set it by Dagon, Dagon their god fell on his face to the earth before the Ark of the Lord (1 Samuel 5:1-7).

The manifestation of His presence to the Church is enough to overcome the enemy's power that seeks to destroy her. We must desperately need the power of God.

When His presence leaves the Church, she becomes empty of His power. This is the reason the devil is in the Church, and will fulfill his mission while the Church remains seated. The preciousness of His power to His Church has made us victorious and over-comers. It is by His power that we, as the Church, conquer the territories and take over our identity, purpose, destiny, and inheritance.

# Chapter 10
## The Identity of the Church in Christ Jesus

*Now I saw a new heaven and a new earth, for the first heaven and earth had passed away. Also, there was no more sea. Then I, John, saw the Holy City, New Jerusalem, coming down out of heaven from God, prepared as a bride adorned for her husband. And I heard a voice from heaven saying, "Behold, the TABERNACLE of God is with me, and He will dwell with them, and they shall be His people. God Himself will be with them and be their God." - Revelation 21:1-3*

The Church of Christ possesses an identity that should portray the likeness of Christ. She is called "His Remnant Church". She knows she is God's dwelling place therefore she is being built into a living and holy sanctuary.

Even though she is still in the process of being molded, she has willingly given herself fully to the Lord God.

She is only found at a place the Lord God has chosen for her. She is hidden in the secret place. This is the Lord's presence (Psalm 27:4). She knows the Lord's foundation is found on His holy mountain (Psalms 87:1).

She is chosen by God as a royal priesthood, a holy nation, a people belonging to Him, that she may declare praises of Him who called her out of darkness. Therefore, she is seeking to take over this full identity. (1 Peter 2:9). She is not running away from the press and the fire because she knows without this she can't be complete (Malachi 3:3), (Zechariah 13:9). She is being cleansed, sanctified, purified, and changed by the Word of God, His pure blood, and His Holy Spirit.

She is not running away from the wilderness, because she knows this is a place for intimacy (Hosea 2:14-20). She is seeking to develop a strong personal relationship that leads to love and intimacy with the Father, because she knows she must conceive and give birth to His fruit (Songs of Solomon 2:4-6), (John 15:4). The fruit of the Spirit, which is love, is being developed within her because she knows she is going nowhere without love for all souls and for the Lord God (Galatians 5:22). She is living in repentance, through seeking righteousness and holiness, for she knows her King is holy and is coming for a holy Church. She is living by the Spirit, because she knows this is the only way she can live and fulfill the will of her Father (Galatians 5:16-17). She is thirsting for Him more than anything else because she knows she is complete with His fullness (Psalm 42:1-2). She is seeking to take after the Lord Jesus Christ's likeness, and so she has surrendered herself to the Holy Spirit, who is transforming her.

Her desire is to reflect the glory of the Lord God, so she knows she must be filled by His Spirit more and more. She is operating in the gifts of the Spirit because she knows this is what brings God the glory (1 Corinthians 12). She is living in repentance because she knows she must be holy as God is holy. She has separated herself for the Lord God because she wants to hear Him, see Him, feel Him, taste of Him, and touch Him. Without separation, she cannot enter into the inner courts. This is the Holy of Holies, where the Ark of the Covenant dwells. She is pressing through the Holy of Holies, to meet and speak with the Lord. It is in between the Cherubim that God told Moses that He would meet with him and speak with Him. It's easy for her to take after God's likeness because she personally knows Him.

There is a special identity she must possess to be the New Jerusalem. She has not only been called, but also chosen by God.

> *But you are a chosen people, a royal priesthood, holy nation, a people belonging to God, that you may declare the praises of Him who called you out of darkness into His wonderful light. - 1 Peter 2:9*

If she knows this, then she desires nothing more than the Lord God. She wants more of Him. **Let's take up our true identity in Christ Jesus!**

# Prayer for the Church

My deepest Prayer for the Church is that:

- The God of our Lord Jesus Christ, the glorious Father, may give you the Spirit of wisdom and revelation, so that you may know Him better (Ephesians 1:17).

- That the eyes of your heart may be enlightened in order that you may know the hope to which He has called you, the riches of His glorious inheritance in His holy people, and His incomparably great power for us who believe (Ephesians 1:18-19).

- YOU SHALL love the house where the Lord lives, the place where His glory dwells (Psalm 26:8).

- Your desire shall be to dwell in the house of the LORD all the days of your life, to gaze on the beauty of the LORD and to seek Him in his temple (Psalm 27:4).

- You shall be transformed into His Likeness with ever-increasing glory, which comes from the Lord, who is the Spirit (2 Corinthians 3:18)

- You may be grounded in Christ's love, and that you may be able to comprehend, with all the saints, the width and length and depth and height -- to know the love of Christ which passes knowledge, that you may be filled with all the fullness of God (Ephesians 3:17-18).

- That your relationship, love, and intimacy with God will grow each day.

Love and Blessings!

# About the Author

Rose Mowriyah Shivambo is a passionate young author, currently serving God as a worshipper, an intercessor, a teacher of His pure Word, and a prophetic minister. She has been called by God and chosen to accomplish a unique purpose in His Kingdom in this end times. She is a B.BIT holder, and currently pursuing her 2nd degree in BSN. She is the founder of QUEENS in Preparation & KINGS in the Making Ministry that seeks to bring God's presence back to His Church. She is also a founder of Fountain of Treasures Foundation Non-profit Organization, a ministry that seeks to support the poor, the orphans, and the widows both spiritually, physically, and economically, fulfilling James 1:27. Her passion is to grow more intimate with the Lord Jesus Christ, and to carry and manifest His presence on earth.

www.ingramcontent.com/pod-product-compliance
Lightning Source LLC
Chambersburg PA
CBHW071331040426
42444CB00009B/2131